MW00611965

Diversity Awareness Activities for Creating a Positive Classroom Environment:

Activity Book for Grades K-12

Edited and Written by
Mark Charles Good

Diversity Awareness Activities for Creating a Positive Classroom Environment:
Activity Book for Grades K-12
By Mark Charles Good

Copyright © 2014 Mark Charles Good
All rights reserved.

Published by Constructive Nonconformity Publishing, LLC.
230 N. 21st Street, Unit 102
Philadelphia, PA 19103
610.733.9402
read@markcharlesgood.com

Author Photograph: Mark Good
Cover Photograph: Create Space

ISBN- 978-0-9913808-2-4

☞ Diversity Awareness activities for use with any K-12 educational discipline.

☞ Categories include:
- Icebreakers
- Defining diversity
- Confronting negative assumptions
- Confronting stereotyping
- Confronting name-calling
- Self-identity in a diverse world
- Effective interpersonal communication
- Celebrating diversity

☞ Step-by-step instructions for each activity.

☞ "How-to-use this book" instructions for each and every k-12 educator.

☞ Glossary of terms categorized by age group.

☞ Table of contents for easy access to the activity you want to use.

Contents

Introduction

Since 1999, I have been teaching a graduate course that I created for educators titled, "Diversity Awareness in Education: A New Perspective for a Changing Classroom." As the world around us changes, so does the student dynamic of our classrooms, offices, libraries, gymnasiums, etc. within our schools.

Subsequently, this course has undergone many changes over the years. As it does, there are interactive activities facilitated in the class that have been helpful in providing k-12 educators a greater awareness and understanding of students as individuals in an ever changing community, whether we believe that community is diverse or homogeneous.

As a result, it seemed important to create an activity book, which provides step-by-step instructions on many of the activities used in this class. Also included, are some activities that I have used in trainings, in-services, and other professional development workshops for k-12 educators who work in any and all disciplines.

I hope you find these activities to be helpful for you as an educator, regardless of the grade level and/or discipline in which you may be employed within the k-12 setting. I also hope that you and your students have lots of fun while creating a dynamic that is welcoming, safe and ripe for learning.

Be Well,
-Mark

*Glossary of Terms

Ages 8 – 12

Assimilate – To become just like everyone else without staying just like you.
Jeff was told to assimilate to the rest of the boys in class.

Assumption – To immediately be certain that someone is the way you believe they are just because of how they look or act.
She made the assumption that he is mean because he has dark brown hair.

Discrimination – To treat someone poorly because of the group to which you believe they belong.
Sometimes there is discrimination against people who are not good at sports.

Gender - the sex of a person or animal.
People of both genders, male and female, enjoy horseback riding.

Homophobia – The belief that people who fall in love with those who are of a different gender are better than those people who fall in love with those who are of the same gender.
Homophobia is the reason Mr. Jacobs thinks Jenny's parents are not as good as Tim's parents.

Prejudice –To negatively judge a person or persons without really knowing them.
There are laws that protect people against acts of prejudice.

Racism – The belief that certain races are better than other races because they were born that way.
Laws that allowed some people and not others to become American citizens in the United States were because of racism.

Scapegoating – To blame other people for your own problems when they are not really to blame.
When the police chief fired the young officer it was because he was scapegoating him.

Stereotyping – To believe that all people who belong to a certain group are the same and will behave in the same way all of the time.
Because his grades were bad, Rich began stereotyping himself and believing that all boys who are good at football are poor students.

Ages 13 – 18

Assimilate – To absorb and incorporate into the dominant culture.
When he started in the new school he was told he needed to assimilate in order to be successful there.

Assumption –to suppose or take for granted that an individual or group of individuals is exactly as we believe they are simply because of the way they look, behave, or what we have heard from others about them. Assumptions are impulsive ideas people have that are not based on proven facts. An assumption can be correct or incorrect.
He made the assumption that she will be unkind simply because she is a police officer.

Discrimination – To treat an individual or members of a group negatively because of the group to which they belong.
The civil rights movement fought to bring an end to discrimination in this country.

Gender - the sex of a person or animal.
People of both genders, male and female, enjoy horseback riding.

Homophobia – The belief that heterosexuality is inherently superior to homosexuality or bisexuality.
Homophobia is the reason Mr. Jacobs thinks Jenny's parents, who happen to be of the same sex, are not equipped to be good parents to Jenny or partners to one another.

Prejudice – Feelings and judgments about an individual or group, which lacks a foundation in fact.
There are laws that protect people against acts of prejudice.

Racism – The belief that a particular race is inherently superior to another race or races.
Laws that allowed some immigrants and not others to become American citizens in the United States were influenced by racism.

Scapegoating –Placing blame upon another person or group for something they did not do in order to justify one's own setbacks.
The police chief fired the officer in question, but the problem in the department was much larger and the young officer was just a scapegoat.

Stereotyping –The belief that all members of the group have all of the same characteristics and therefore always behave alike.

The team captain was failing in school, and he was sadly convinced that he fit the stereotype of the dumb athlete.

* The definitions of the terms used in this book, are defined in a way that is specific to the relevancy of this book. (E.g., "Discrimination" is defined in relation to people vs. objects.) In other words, a child may discriminate between a hot stove vs. a cold stove after she touches a hot stove and burns her hand. This is an example of discrimination based upon an object. People are more complex. In other words, they may not always respond or act in a predictable and consistent manner, as does an object such as a stove. Therefore, the definition of discrimination in this book pertains to people.

How To Use This Activity Booklet

The Activity
[The Name of the Activity]

Objective: [The primary purpose of this activity.

For: *[The age range for whom this activity is most appropriate. These age ranges are simply a guideline. You may find that any of the activities in the book can be modified in order to be used with students of all age ranges.]*

Time Needed: *[The approximate time needed to complete this activity. Times will vary based on size of group and modifications the facilitator decides to make.]*

Number of Participants: *[The minimum to maximum number of individuals for whom this activity is appropriate.]*

Materials Needed: *[The physical materials that the facilitator will need in order to complete the activity.]*

Set Up: *[Suggestion(s) for arrangements before beginning the activity.]*

Directions: *[The step-by-step process for facilitating the activity. Feel free to modify in any way that may be more appropriate for your students.]*

Key Points: *[Important information for the instructor to consider or point out to the students who participate.]*

> **IMPORTANT:** Emotional and physical safety are of the utmost importance for all activities. No activity in this book is guaranteed to reach the desired results. However, carefully assessing your audience will be beneficial to overall results.

ICEBREAKERS

Equity Autographs

Objective: To allow groups that do not know each other well or do not know each other based on certain personal aspects of one another's lives to interact without great risk.

For: Ages 7 - Adult

Time Needed: 15 minutes

Number of Participants: 10 - 50

Materials Needed:
- "Equity Autograph" worksheet (found on next page)
- A writing utensil for each participant

Set Up:

Large enough space for participants to be able to walk around the room and interact.

Directions:

To the large group: "Find other people in this room who match the descriptions in any of the twenty that are listed on your worksheet. You must find a different person for each description. Have each person sign his/her initials in the blank space next to the description he/she matches. When you have found ten different people (you can make this less or more than ten), contact the teacher immediately."

The instructor/teacher may wish to provide a prize for the individual who completes the exercise first and correctly.

Key Points: Let the student know that this activity allows them to know each other in a way that they may have not before.

Equity Autographs Worksheet

Find individuals who match the descriptions of any ten of the statements below. You must find a different person for each. Have each person sign his/her initials in the appropriate space next to the description that he/she matches. When you have found ten different individuals, contact the instructor/teacher immediately.

_____1. Has a sister.

_____2. Has a brother.

_____3. Has a parent from a different state.

_____4. Can speak more than one language.

_____5. Celebrates Diwali.

_____6. Celebrates Passover.

_____7. Celebrates Christmas.

_____8. Celebrates Ramadan.

_____9. Is left-handed.

_____10. Is a vegetarian.

_____11. Has a neighbor of a different race.

_____12. Has been to Alaska.

_____13. Has traveled outside the U.S. A.

_____14. Has two dogs as pets.

_____15. Has a cat as a pet.

_____16. Has lived in a city.

_____17. Whose favorite color is blue.

_____18. Goes to the movies once a month.

_____19. Whose doctor is a woman.

_____20. Lives with someone older than 70.

© MarkCharlesGood, LLC.

Birthday Line-Up

Objective:
- To begin to understand the importance of communication within diversity

For: 7 – Adult

Time Needed: 10-15 minutes

Number of Participants: Entire student body working together.

Materials Needed:
- An area large enough for students to be able to line up next to one another while standing

Set Up:
- Have students line up in no specific order, shoulder to shoulder, facing in one direction, and in an area of the room that allows for such an activity.

Directions:
- After having the students line up, the instructor should stand before them and then state to the large group: "I am going to ask you to line up in a specific order. I am going to ask you to line up in order of birthday. That means, please line up in order of month and day - not year. I would like the person whose birthday is closest to January 1st to line up at this end of the line (point to your right which will be to the students' left). The person whose birthday is closest to December 31st will line up at this end of the line (point to your left which will be to the students' right). *However*, you must line up in this order *without* speaking. Are there any questions?" Answer questions then state, "Okay, you may begin."

- After the students have lined up, ask the large group: "Would you like to make any changes before we see what you have come up with? (Pause) Okay, let's start at the end of the line closest to January 1st and ask each of you to state your birthday. If you find that you are in the incorrect order, please just place yourself in the correct spot when you learn where that is." It's important to include this last sentence as it will include an *objective question that you will be asking at the conclusion of this activity.
- After the students have stated their birthdays, ask the following questions:
  - What helped you to do this well?
    - Some answers may include: 'a common language where we used our fingers; previous knowledge of our calendar here in the western part of the world; etc.'
  - What hindered you from getting this done more quickly or exactly right?
    - Some answers may include: 'not being able to speak; confusion with the *language* we were using; etc.'
  - Now that you have lined up in the correct chronological order, do you have this completed *exactly right*?
    - The answer should be: 'Yes'
    - State that, "the answer is 'yes' because it is an objective, measurable (something that has only one answer) activity to complete. And that practicing diversity is not always this objective or measurable".

Key Points: This activity is a preview for understanding that 'diversity' is not always as objective or as measurable (something that has only one answer) as many other topics within school.

Personal Artifacts

Objective:
- For students to begin with an activity that helps to create a lasting sense of community and the importance of appreciating diversity.
- For students to understand that all of us has a personal story that is relevant and important.

For: 6 – Adult

Time Needed: 20 – 90 minutes (depending on the size of the group)

Number of Participants: Entire student body. Each student sharing a personal story with the rest of the class.

Materials Needed:
- One personal artifact from each student
- Artifact – In this activity, we will define "artifact" as an "object" or "item".

Set Up:
- Desks or tables in a circle with students facing toward the inside of the circle.
- The instructor should sit among the students in the circle of desks or tables.

Directions:
- Ask the large group: "Please consider the following: Let's say that you were told that you must leave your home and that you will never be allowed to return to it. You are told that in addition to the people and pets with whom you may be living, you are allowed to only take one inanimate (non-living) object with you and nothing else. This object is a *personal artifact* that is very important to you. It is not necessarily important to you because of its

monetary value (it is worth money) but because of it sentimental value (how it makes you feel). What would be that one *personal artifact* that you would choose to take?"

- IMPORTANT: Let the students know that there is one restriction. No one is allowed to choose a *personal artifact* that is a photograph unless it represents what is important to you. In others words, please do not simply bring in a family photo.

- Assign the students: To bring that *personal artifact* with them during an upcoming class. During that class they will be asked to do the following three things:
  - Show us the *personal artifact.*
  - Tell us what it is.
  - Tell us why it is so important to you.

- You will be given as much time as you need to tell us your story (you may also wish to set time limits based on your scheduling limitations).

Key Points:

- After each student has had a chance to disclose, point out that if we were to place every *personal artifact* into the center of our circle and then asked someone outside of the class 'how much money would you give us for all of them?' That person might not offer us very much.

- However, after hearing each person's personal story, we all know that each of those *personal artifacts* alone is truly priceless.

- Point out that each person with whom we come in contact, even that one person who drives you crazy, likely also has a *personal artifact* and a personal story that is priceless to him/her and that no single artifact or story is more important than another. By keeping this in mind, we may be able to understand that each of us is important and connected to one another in some way, no matter how different we see ourselves from one another.

DEFINING DIVERSITY

The Diversity Iceberg

Objective: To create a definition of "diversity" that is relevant to those participating.

For: 12 – Adult

Time Needed: 15 minutes

Number of Participants: Entire student body working in small groups.

Materials Needed:
- Pen or magic marker.
- A piece of blank paper and a writing utensil for each small group.

Set Up:
- Situated into small groups of no more than 6 per small group.
- Each small group should assign a recorder and a reporter.

Directions:
- To the Large Group:
  - Ask students if they know what the word "diversity" means. Some answers might include, "difference", "different races", or "different ways of life."
  - Have students draw a "Diversity Iceberg" that looks like the one on the page following these instructions. You can also copy the worksheet on the next page and distribute one copy to each group.
  - Tell them that it is an iceberg and like the characteristics of any iceberg, what we see is only the tip of the iceberg. The largest part of the iceberg is located below the water line where we cannot see it.

- Tell the large group that in the late 1980's and early 1990's when the topic of diversity was first included as an important topic, that only two primary topics were discussed.
- These two topics were "race" and "gender" (written on the picture) and as they are situated on the picture, both are those things we can easily see. As a result, they are written above the water line at the top of the iceberg.
- Tell the large group that today we now include much more within the topic of diversity. Those things we can see (like race and gender) and those things we cannot see and would be written on our picture below the water.
- Ask for an example of something that is part of diversity that we cannot see that might be placed below the water around the iceberg. Some answers might include "political beliefs", "socioeconomic status", "sexual orientation", or "religious beliefs".
- To Small Groups:
  - Direct the large group to now work in their small groups to write down as many areas of diversity they can think of that can be written above *and* below the water. Those things we can see *and* cannot see.
  - If it may assist the students, you can ask them to consider the first day of school and seeing their fellow students enter into the classroom on that first day.
  - Ask if they have any questions, respond, then direct them to take their time and begin.
  - After all of the small groups have finished, ask them to do the following:

- "Please post or display your iceberg's on the wall (or hold them up)."
- "As you look at each group's iceberg, what are some of the things that stand out to you or that you notice is common among all or most of the icebergs?"
- Some responses may include:
  - A very large list.
  - A lot of groups came up with the same ones.
  - *Important: Many or most of what was written is below the water.*
- Tell the large group that all of these answers are correct.
- *That like an iceberg, most of what diversity includes are those things we cannot see and is located below the water.*
- Then also point out that as they look at the entire picture they will most likely see that there are several areas of diversity in which they could find themselves included.

Key Points:

- Not only does diversity include several areas; many or most areas are things we cannot see when we look at a person.
- As a result, we are all a part of diversity.
- In other words, *Diversity* is about *"the inclusion of all and the exclusion of none."*

Diversity Iceberg

Race

Gender

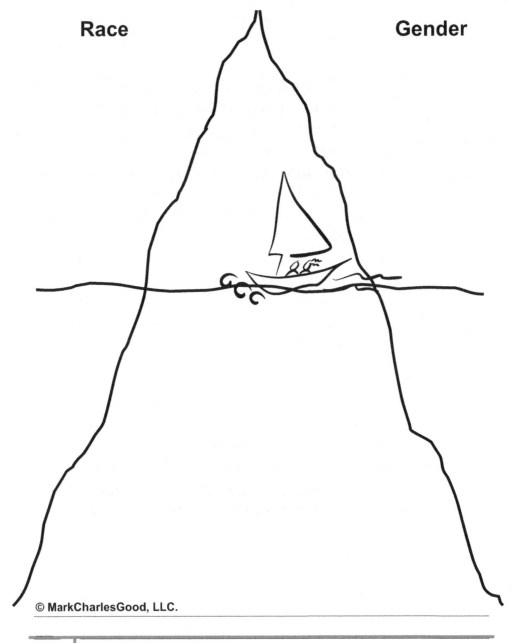

© MarkCharlesGood, LLC.

Eyeshade Line-Up

Objective:

- To show that practicing diversity is not always measurable with one answer for every group.
- To reinforce the importance of communication within diversity.
- To reinforce that in order for diversity initiatives to work we must use the assistance of others to come up with our best answers.
- To reinforce the importance that discomfort is congruent with positive change.

For: 9 – Adult

Time Needed: 10-15 minutes

Number of Participants: Entire student body working together.

Materials Needed:

- An area large enough for students to be able to line up next to one another while standing.

Set Up:

- Have students line up in no specific order, shoulder to shoulder, facing in one direction, and in an area of the room that allows for such an activity just as they did previously with the *Birthday Line-Up Activity*.

Directions:

- <u>After having the students line up, stand before them and then state to the large group</u>: "I would like to ask you to line up in a specific order again and again without speaking. But this time, I am not going to ask you to line up in order of *birthday*, but instead in order of *eyeshade* – not eye color (e.g., blue, brown, green). I would like the person whose *eyeshade is the darkest* to line up at this end of the line (point to your right which will be to the students' left). The person whose *eyeshade is the lightest* to line up at this end of the line (point to your left which will be to the students' right). Again, please line up in this order *without* speaking. Any questions? (Pause) Okay, you may begin."

- After the students have lined up, ask the large group the following questions:
  o "Would you like to make any changes before we see what you have come up with? (Pause)
  o How is this activity different from the *Birthday Activity*?
    ▪ Some answers may include: "this activity is more subjective"; "we needed other people to help us come up with the answer"; "we needed to get physically close to each other"; etc.
  o Now that you have lined up in this order, do you have this completed *exactly right*?
    ▪ The answer should be: 'No' because it is a subjective activity and not measurable (there is not only one right answer).

Key Points:
Tell the students that this activity is activity looks a lot more like 'diversity' than the *Birthday Activity* because:
  o It is more subjective.
  o They needed to work with others to come up with the best answer.
  o Communication that may be uncomfortable due to close physical proximity must take place in order to be successful.

- o There is no one answer for every group. Each group may have a different answer, which is the best answer for them.
- o After stating the key points, have the students return to their small groups and follow-up with "The Comfort Circle."

The Comfort Circle

Objective: To illustrate that discomfort is congruent with positive change.
For: 9 - Adult
Time Needed: 10 minutes
Number of Participants: Presentation to entire student body.
Materials Needed:
  ▪ Blackboard/Whiteboard or large piece of paper.
  ▪ Writing utensil for instructor.
Set Up:
  ▪ Students sitting in small groups or large group to watch instructor.

Directions:
  • Draw the **Diagram 1.** ("comfort circle" on the next page) for each of the students to see.
  • To large group: "Each of us has a *comfort circle*. We are placed within the middle of that circle. Each time we experience something new that creates discomfort, it takes place outside our *comfort circle*. Place a dot outside the circle that is written on the board/paper in front of the class (Diagram 2.).
  • Then say, "However, despite the fact that this experience creates discomfort and takes place outside the circle, it helps our *comfort circle* to become larger."
  • Draw a larger circle around the second dot (Diagram 3.).
  • Then say, "Subsequently, anytime we experience something that was originally outside our *comfort*

circle, now it takes place within a new and larger *comfort circle*."

Key Points: Those who are unwilling to try new things due to a fear of discomfort will always possess a small *comfort circle*, correlating with a small worldview and a great deal of difficulty managing diversity within their lives.

Comfort Circle

Diagram 1.

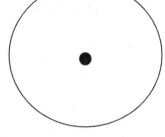

Diagram 2.

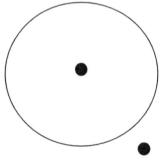

Diagram 3.

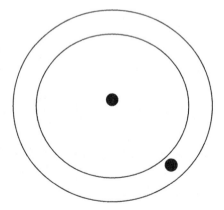

© MarkCharlesGood, LLC.

CONFRONTING NEGATIVE ASSUMPTIONS

Negative Assumptions Can Hurt Everyone

Objective: To illustrate the importance of confronting *negative assumptions* before they can lead to negative forms of stereotyping, prejudice, discrimination, racism/homophobia, scapegoating and genocide.

For: Ages 7 - Adult

Time needed: 15 minutes (10 minutes for video and 5 minutes to display "dangerous process")

Number of Participants: 3 - 40

Materials Needed:
- "The Lunch Date" found on YouTube at **http://www.youtube.com/watch?v=epuTZigxUY8**

Set Up:
- Situated into small groups of no more than 5 per small group.

Directions:
- To the large group:
  - Ask the large group if someone can give an example of a "negative assumption" then after that has been answered ask if someone else can give an example of a "positive assumption". You can always provide the definition of "assumption" (found in the "Glossary" section of this book) if you feel that would be appropriate for the age group.
  - Tell the students that you are going to show them a 10-minute video titled "The Lunch Date".
  - Tell them that as they watch the video you would like them to write down or think about any assumptions, positive or negative, they may have about the main female character

in the video and the main male character in the video.

- Then tell them to look closely because there is a surprise ending and you would like to have them see if any of their assumptions may have changed as a result.

- After the video is over tell them that no matter what our assumptions might have been about the characters we still do not know if any of them are correct unless we knew them as individuals.

- It's the same way with anyone we come in contact with here in school or outside of school.

- Finally tell the students that if we do not think about questioning our own assumptions it <u>might</u> lead to our stereotyping others and feeling prejudice toward them.

- This activity can be followed-up by "The Pebble Exercise" on stereotyping (found in the "Confronting Stereotyping" section of this book).

Key Points: To help participants understand that it is important to look within ourselves before judging others and that the only way we know for sure as to whether our assumptions are correct is if we get to know someone first.

The Fishbowl

Objective: To reinforce the importance of the fact that each of us has our own perspective on the world around us, and to increase empathy among students.

For: 7 – Adult

Time Needed: 30-60 minutes (you can repeat as often as you wish)

Number of Participants: Entire student body working individually then in small groups and finally with the instructor as a large group.

Materials Needed:

- Approximately 6-8 chairs or desks placed in a circle in the middle of the room.
- The rest of the group sitting outside the circle as observers.

Set Up:

Survey the students to find out if any of the following are in the class (note: these are just a few of the characteristics that you can use. Add as many to the list that you feel would be appropriate for your group). It is also important to determine the level of risk you wish to reach with this activity. Some characteristics may be too threatening for some students to want to share:

- Someone who likes to be alone.
- Someone who is shy.
- Someone who sometimes gets picked on.
- Someone who gets called names and it hurts my feelings.
- Someone who often feels different from others.
- Someone who is different "than people think I am."
- Someone who does something outside of school that nobody knows about and of which I am proud.

Directions:

Instructor tells large group:
- Those <u>Outside</u> the Fishbowl:
- *During* the discussion:
    - Please do not speak or ask questions of those inside the fishbowl.
    - Please listen carefully to what each person in the fishbowl has to say.
- Immediately *After* the discussion:
    - Write down your observations regarding commonalities among and important points made by those inside the fishbowl made.
- Those <u>Inside</u> the Fishbowl:
- *During* the discussion:
    - Please only speak about yourself.
    - Please do not ask questions of anyone inside or outside the fishbowl.
    - Please, no putting down others.
- Immediately *After* the discussion:
    - Write down what it felt like to participate inside the fishbowl.

Small Groups:
- After the final fishbowl has completed their discussion, ask the students to work in their small groups to answer these three questions and either write them down on a large piece of paper or a small piece of paper and then on the board:
    - "How can this activity be helpful to you?"
    - "How can this activity be helpful to others?"
    - "How could we change this activity so that everyone might feel willing to be speak openly while in the fishbowl?"

Large Group:
- Share responses

Key Points:

- To become better able to practice empathy in all situations.
- To help create a welcoming and safe environment for all students by understanding the plight of others.

CONFRONTING STEREOTYPING

The Pebble Exercise

Objective: To introduce the concept of stereotyping and to illustrate how our generalizations can influence our thinking about people.

For: 5 – Adult

Time needed: 15 minutes

Number of Participants: Entire student body working in small groups.

Materials Needed:

- 1 pebble for each small group (5-10 total). [Note: you can use other objects for this activity, such as lemons. Pebbles work well because they are non-perishable.)
- 1 writing utensil for each small group.
- 1 piece of blank paper per group.
- PPT entitled *"Characteristics of Pebbles"* OR whiteboard/smartboard.
- Chalk/dry erase marker.

Set Up:

- Situated into small groups of no more than 5 per small group.
- Each small group should assign a recorder and a reporter.

Directions:

- Place the entire group of pebbles in plain view for all students to see.
- Ask all of the students to list "the characteristics of pebbles" (e.g. smooth, hard, etc.) out loud.
- As students begin to list the characteristics, write them on the whiteboard/smartboard. Then

read the entire list to the students when completed (a list of no more than 15 is good).

- Give each small group a pebble or have someone from each group (other than the recorder or reporter) come to the front of the room to choose a pebble for their group.
- Instruct each group to work together to describe the physical characteristics and history (a fun made up story) of their particular pebble. Give each group five minutes or less to do this.
- After each group has finished, have a member of the group return their pebble to the front of the room where they originally picked up the pebble. Then mix the pebble up so that they are in a different position than where they were when returned.
- Ask each group to pick a new person who has not yet participated.
- She/he will come to the front of the room to find the group's particular pebble again. This is usually easy for the student to do since each group has already had an opportunity to get to know their specific pebble as an individual rather than as a member of a group. It is okay if the student asks for help from the other students from the small group.
- Ask the students:
  - "Why do you think it was so easy to find your own pebble so quickly?"
  - "What do you think was the purpose of this exercise?"
  - Some responses might include: "Because we got to know our pebble as an individual." or "Because it became our own special pebble."

Key Points:

- The point of this exercise is to illustrate how easy it is for us to place individuals who we see as members of a group (e.g. racial; gender; intelligence; sexual orientation; etc.) into categories without looking at them as individuals first.
- When we do this with objects such as the pebble it can be accepted. But when we do it with people it can be dangerous, as it is known as stereotyping.

The Challenge Contract
(Ages 5 – 8)

Objective: To challenge students to practice confronting their own personal stereotyping.

For: 5 – 8

Number of Participants: 3 - 50

Materials Needed:
- "Challenge Contract" worksheet, one for each student (on next page).
- Writing utensil for each student.

Time needed: 10 – 15 minutes

Set Up:
- Students working individually at desks or tables.

Directions:
- Tell the students that you would like to present a challenge to them.
- Instruct the students something like this, "Next time you are in a place that you attend frequently (cafeteria, the hallway, class, a party or dance) try something that might be new to you. Search for a person or a group of people that you believe is quite different from you and that you really don't know very well. You may believe this difference exists between you as a result of what you have seen yourself or what you have heard from your friends.
- Have the student single out (to themselves only) one person from that so called, "different group". After they have chosen that person, ask the students to "begin to observe him/her

whenever you have the opportunity, but as discreetly as possible so as not to startle the person.

- Start to notice that person's individual characteristics that set him/her apart from anyone else. Look at characteristics that might be physical characteristics; mannerisms; sense of humor; emotions. Maybe even begin to think about his/her life outside of school and his/her past or his/her goals for the future."

- When the students have done this for part of the day ask them to make an attempt to approach that person sometime within the near future and talk to the person. <u>While remembering not to choose a person who initiates concerns for their safety</u>.

- Consider trying to do <u>any</u> of the following with that person for not less than ten minutes: walking to class together; eating lunch together; asking about his/her weekend; just saying 'hello' and sincerely asking "How are you doing?" apologizing to someone that they may have been unkind to; if having an unfair feeling about a person from a particular racial group, gender, sexual orientation, etc. they will try to find out more about their positive contributions to my country, etc.

- Instruct the students to search for commonalities rather than differences. Tell them that although there will probably be differences between the two of them, just getting to know that person as an individual rather than as a member of the group will most likely begin to breakdown stereotypes about that person and his/her 'group'.

Challenge Contract

By completing and signing my name to this contract, I have made a promise to myself to act on what I have learned about stereotyping people.

By doing so, I promise myself to do one kind thing by either choosing one of the ideas that were given by my teacher or choosing another that I think is important.

My contract to myself is to

_____
_____
_____
_____
_____
_____
_____
_____
_____
_____

by_____
     DATE

Signed_____
      NAME

© MarkCharlesGood, LLC.

The Challenge Contract
(Ages 9 – Adult)

Objective: To challenge students to practice confronting their own personal stereotyping.
For: 9 – Adult
Number of Participants: 3 - 50
Materials Needed:
- "Challenge Contract" worksheet, one for each student (on next page).
- Writing utensil for each student.

Time needed: 10 – 15 minutes
Set Up:
- Students working individually at desks or tables.

Directions:
- Tell the students that you would like to present a challenge to them.
- Instruct the students something like this, "Next time you are in a place that you attend frequently (cafeteria, the hallway, class, the bus, the locker room, a party or a dance, even on Facebook) try something that might be new to you."
- "Search for a person or a group of people that you believe are quite different from you and that you really don't know very well. You may believe this difference exists between you as a result of what you have seen yourself or what you have heard from others.'
- "Then choose one person from that so called, "different group" to concentrate on. Do not to tell them or anyone that you have done this.

After you have chosen that person, begin to observe him/her whenever you have the opportunity, but kindly so as not to startle the person."

- Start to notice that person's individual characteristics that set her/him apart from anyone else. Look at characteristics that might be physical; mannerisms; sense of humor; emotions."
- "Maybe even begin to think about his/her life outside of school and his/her past or his/her goals for the future."
- When the students have done this for a period of a few days (or part of one day) ask them to make an attempt to approach that person sometime within the near future and talk to the person. <u>While remembering not to choose a person who initiates concerns for their safety</u>.
- Consider trying to do <u>any</u> of the following with that person for not less than ten minutes: walking to class together; eating lunch together; asking about his/her weekend; just saying 'hello' and sincerely asking "how are you doing?" apologizing to someone that they may have been unkind to; if having an unfair feeling about a person from a particular racial group, gender, sexual orientation, etc. they will try to find out more about their positive contributions to my country, etc.
- Instruct the students to search for commonalities rather than differences. Tell them that although there will probably be differences between the two of them, just getting to know that person as an individual rather than as a member of the group will most

likely begin to break down stereotypes about that person and his/her 'group'.

Challenge Contract

By completing and signing my name to this contract, I have made a commitment to act on what I have learned regarding the danger of stereotyping people.

By doing so, I promise myself to perform at least one kind act by either choosing one of the suggestions that were given by the teacher or choosing another that I think is important.

My contract to myself is to

_____

_____

_____

_____

_____

_____

_____

_____

_____

_____

by_____
      DATE

Signed_____
          NAME

© MarkCharlesGood, LLC.

CONFRONTING NAME-CALLING

Angry Words Remain

Objective: A story that assists students in comprehending how words matter.

For: 5 – Adult

Number of Participants: 3 - 50

Materials Needed:
- "Angry Words Remain" story (on next page).

Time needed: 5 - 10 minutes

Set Up:
- Large group listening to teacher read.

Directions:
- Read the short story found on the next page to your students.
- Ask them what the lesson is they believe the story has offered.
- List responses on paper, whiteboard, or smartboard.

Key Points:
- A verbal wound can be as bad as a physical one.

ANGRY WORDS REMAIN

There once was a little boy who had a bad temper. His father gave him a bag of nails and told him that every time he lost his temper, he must hammer a nail into the back of the fence. The first day the boy had driven 37 nails into the fence. Over the next few weeks, as he learned to control his anger, the number of nails hammered daily gradually dwindled down. He discovered it was easier to hold his temper than to drive those nails into the fence. Finally, the day came when the boy did not lose his temper at all.

He told his father about it and the father suggested that the boy now pull out one nail for each day that he was able to hold his temper. The day passed and the young boy was finally able tell his father that all the nails were gone.

The father took his son by the hand and led him to the fence. He said, "You have done well, my son, but look at the holes in the fence. The fence will never be the same. When you say things in anger, they leave a scar just like this one. You can put a knife in a man and draw it out. It won't matter how many times you say I'm sorry, the wound is still there."

© MarkCharlesGood, LLC.

The Pain We Have Felt
The Hurt We Have Caused

Objective: For students to comprehend how painful name-calling can be to ourselves and to others and to begin an initiative to end it in your classroom.

For: 5 – Adult

Number of Participants: 3 - 50

Materials Needed:
- Give each student a 3x5 index card.
- A 2nd set of colored index cards.
- Writing utensil for each student.

Time needed: 45 – 60 minutes

Set Up:
- Participants working individually at desks or tables.
- Then working together as a large group.

Directions:

To the large group:
- Tell the students there should be no talking during this part of the activity (to avoid jokes and competition).
- Ask them to then close their eyes and remember a time when someone called you a name. Do your best to remember and feel exactly what happened.
- Write down the specifics of the event and the name you were called on the index card. Underline the name you were called.
- Do not write your name on the card. I will now collect each card.
- I will now give each of you a different colored index card.

- Now think about a time when you called someone else a name. Write down the name you called someone else on the index card and then underline it.
- Write down the specifics of the event and the name you called them.
- When finished, collect these cards.
- Read aloud some of *the Pain We Have Felt* cards to the students. These will reveal deep distress and hurt some of the students have felt.
- Then read aloud some of *the Hurt We Have Caused* cards to the students.
- As a class, take some time to discuss the impact, situations and/or emotions felt by any of the written statements. IMPORTANT: Also consider pointing out that some words themselves do not have meanings that are bad (e.g., "gay") but some people have used it incorrectly to make it mean something that it is not.
- Randomly, redistribute all of the cards to the students.
- Instruct the students to color and draw the underlined words in a way that depicts the ugliness of the emotions they felt about them and discussed as a large group.
- If desired, place some of the finished drawings on a bulletin board in the room for the remainder of the year in order to remind the students of your guidelines that these are words that are not allowed to be used to hurt each other's feelings.

Hurtful Words

Objective: To understand how we are all affected by derogatory name-calling.

For: 5 – Adult

Time Needed: 20 - 30 minutes

Number of Participants: Entire student body working in small groups.

Materials Needed:

- Whiteboard/Blackboard or smartboard.
- Chalk/dry erase marker
- Blank piece of paper for each small group.
- Writing utensil for each small group.
- "Categories" handout for each small group (on next page).
- Clock or watch.

Set Up:

- Situated into small groups of no more than 5 per small group.
- Each small group should assign a recorder.

Directions:

- To the large group: "During this next activity you will be working in your small groups. You will need to have one blank piece of paper, a writing utensil and one person who is to be assigned as a recorder for your small group. NOTE: *Do not yet distribute the "Categories" handout to the class at this point.*
- To the small groups: "For the next three minutes please brainstorm all of the names that students call each other to hurt one another's feelings. Please say them out loud so that the recorder in your small group can write them

down on the blank piece of paper. I know that for some of you this activity may be uncomfortable because of the language but please do your best to participate."

- <u>After three minutes has passed</u>: Ask the small groups to now take all of the words on the paper and make a 'top ten' list. In other words, have them rank in order the words that they hear students call each other the most. Number one will be the most widely used while number ten will be the tenth most widely used. Give them approximately five minutes to complete this part of the activity.

- <u>After five minutes have passed</u>: Now handout the "Categories" handout to each small group. Direct each small group to categorize their top ten list under the words which best describe them. <u>NOTE</u>: Be sure to ask the students to categorize them based on what the words truly mean, NOT what the students claim they mean. In other word, a student may call another student "gay" and claim that it has nothing to do with "sexual orientation". But the small group should categorize it under "sexual orientation" anyway.

- <u>After each group has established categories</u>: Direct each small group to display their final list of categories.

- <u>When completed</u>: After, ask the following to the large group: "Place yourself in the shoes of one of your fellow students. Does a k-12 student **choose** his/her **race**?"

  - The correct answer should be "no".

- <u>Ask this same question for all of the categories listed</u>: For all or most, the likely answer will be "no".

- Then point out: "If we cannot **choose** any of these, then does that not mean that each of us can become the recipient of this hurtful name-calling? And if we can all become recipients of this name-calling, then why do we call others these names?"

Key Points:
- Interestingly, k – 12 students respond well to this explanation when they begin to comprehend how hurtful these words can be.
- Additionally, it is helpful to point out to students that although educators will allow them to say these words out loud for this exercise, you would not like to hear the words used in your class any longer. Again, students welcome an opportunity to enhance safety and respect through such an exercise.

- IMPORTANT: There may be a disagreement or discussion about whether or not k – 12 students can truly choose to be a part of any of the categories listed. One example where this discussion takes place is about "sexual orientation". The instructor can point out that although we may not all agree on whether or not some of these are choices, any educator has the right and responsibility to confront such language and to direct students not to use the words in his/her class, office, library, gymnasium, etc.

Categories

Race

Gender

Religion

Wealth

Sexual Orientation

Physical

Brain

Appearance

Other

© MarkCharlesGood, LLC.

SELF- IDENTITY IN A DIVERSE WORLD

Personal Identity Molecule

VERY IMPORTANT:
- _**This activity should be done <u>before</u> you begin discussing the topic of diversity and/or race.**_
- _**This activity should be followed-up by the "Growing Up Racially" activity which is the next activity in this book.**_

<u>Objective:</u> to prepare students for a very important activity on racial identity and worldview that will take place later.
<u>For:</u> 13 – Adult
<u>Time Needed:</u> 5-10 minutes
<u>Number of Participants:</u> 3 – 30
<u>Materials Needed:</u>
- "Personal Identity Molecule" worksheet, one for each student (on next page).
- Writing utensil for each student.

<u>Set Up:</u> Students working individually and then as a large group.

<u>Directions:</u>
- <u>Distribute </u>"Personal Identity Molecule" worksheet to the students, one for each student.
- <u>To the large group</u>: "Please look at your "Personal Identity Molecule". You will see a large circle surrounded by five smaller circles. This is an activity that you will be doing individually and that at no time during this course, will you be asked to **specifically** share what you write on this page with anyone else <u>unless you wish to do so</u>. In the large circle, please write your name. You can write your first name or your first and last name."

- Give them a few seconds to complete this then state to the large group: "Now, in the five smaller circles please write five groups or categories with which you identify that you believe are *very* important to your *personal* identity. In other words, if I were to look at your name written in the large circle but did not know you very well, what you write in the five smaller circles would help me to get to know you better. That is because the five groups with which you identify are very important to you and you believe, help to make up the important aspects of your personal identity. There are no restrictions to what you can write, one in each circle, and there are no right or wrong answers. Take your time. You have about 5 minutes."

- When each person has finished, state to the large group: "Now, please put this away. However, I promise you that we will be coming back to this later and that there is a good reason as to why we did this activity at the very first."

Key Points:

- It is important to make this last point above so that sequential learners do not feel frustrated.

Personal Identity Molecule

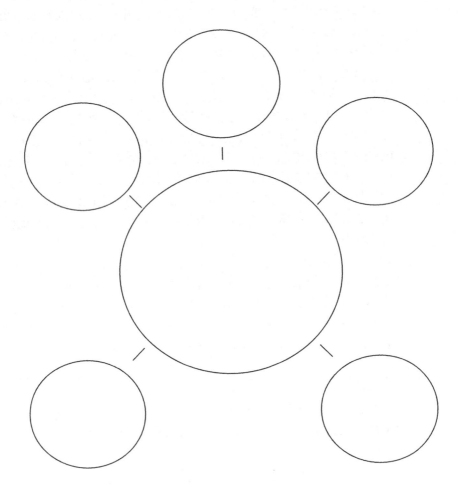

- Write your name in the center circle.
- In the other 5 circles write the name of five groups or categories with which you identify and that you believe are very important to your personal identity.

© MarkCharlesGood, LLC.

"Growing Up Racially" Worksheet & Completion of The "Personal Identity Molecule"

Objective:
- A follow-up to the "Personal Identity Molecule" activity.
- Comprehending that racial perspectives may differ greatly and that there is no right way or wrong way but many ways to possess these perspectives.

For: 13 – Adult

Time Needed: 30 – 45 minutes

Number of Participants: 3 – 30

Materials Needed:
- "Growing Up Racially" worksheet (on next page).
- Writing utensil for each student.

Set Up:
- Students working individually and then as a large group.

Directions:
- Distribute "Growing Up Racially" worksheet to the students, one for each student.
- Ask the large group: "Please look at your "Growing Up Racially" worksheet."
- Direct the group: "Please **work individually** to answer each of the following to the best of your ability."
- VERY IMPORTANT: Be sure to read the directions out loud to the class at the top of the page AND to point out that the questions MUST be answered based on RACE not on ethnicity, religion or any other category. (You may need to define racial groups to the students beforehand as

classified by the U.S. Government. A good resource for this is the U.S. Census (**http://www.census.gov/population/race/**).

- **IMPORTANT**: NEVER classify a student based upon what you or anyone else believes he/she is. Allow each student to classify her/himself only. Stress the importance of this verbally to the class.
- When each student has completed the page, ask the large group: "If I had given you all the time you needed, how many of would have never been able to answer all of these?" (pause).
- Then ask: "Please take a look around the room at how many have raised their hands."
- If the students have completed the assignment correctly, you will likely see that *most white students* have raised their hands.
  - Follow with asking the large group: "If I had given you all the time you needed, how many of you would have been able to answer all of these?" (pause).
  - Then ask: "Please take a look around the room at how many have raised their hands."
    - If the students have completed the assignment correctly, you may see that *many students of color*, especially African-American students have raised their hands.
  - Then process question #4 by asking: "Among those of you who found these questions *not very difficult* to answer, whom would be willing to share with us your answer to #4?"

Key Points:

- If there are **white** students in the class who answer the question based upon **race**, they may have come from a background where messages about **whites related to superiority over other racial groups (or very rarely,**

because there were major discussions about being anti-racist in the home).

- If there are **students of color, especially African-American students** in the class who answer the question based upon **race**, they may have come from a background where messages about **people of color related to survival or safety in a society that was not predominantly "like" them**, not about superiority.

- NOTE: *Most white students who answer these questions without difficulty, will likely answer the questions incorrectly because they will not answer based upon race but instead, based upon characteristics such as simple values, religion or ethnicity. This is because 'well – intentioned' whites are taught not to see race as a part of their identity. As a result, they may be doing a disservice to those students who do see race as an important part of their own identity in a non-racist way.*

- Follow-up with going back to the **"Personal Identity Molecule"** by asking the large group: "Now, please turn back to page 1 in your course booklet. Let's take a look at what you wrote on your "Personal Identity Molecule". As I said on the first day of class, I will not ask any of you to share your specific answers. However, I will ask all of you to raise your hand if I do mention a category that you did write about.

- Follow with asking the large group: "For instance, within the five smaller circles, if any of you wrote something about your profession or career, please raise your hand (pause).

- Then ask: "Please take a look around the room at how many have raised their hands."
- Then do the same with the following categories: "Please raise your hand if you wrote anything relating to your":
  - Job, career or profession
  - Family
  - Faith, spirituality, or religion
  - Hobbies or interests
- Finally ending with: "Please raise your hand if you wrote anything relating to your **race (not your ethnicity).**"

NOTE: *It may be likely you will notice that only the persons of color, especially African – Americans will have raised their hands. This solidifies the 'worldview' that many whites in America do not see their race as an important part of their personal identity while many persons of color do. As a result, it is important for all of us to be aware of and to appreciate the 'worldview' of those who see as member of a different race so that we can better serve, communicate and live with each other in a more peaceful world. No 'worldview' is more correct than another only different from one another.*

You may wish to point out that because of this, when persons of color have frequent discussions of race it is because they may be reminded regularly, by what they see, that they are the member of a race and not often part of the so-called racial majority. And that when whites claim to be color-blind it is because they are taught that is what ant-racists whites should aspire to be. Neither perspective is based upon bigotry, but instead, very different perspectives on the same landscape and based only on race. There are certainly many other perspectives on perceiving the world; race is just one very poignant perspective in our society.

Growing Up Racially

This questionnaire is designed to help you identify **verbal** messages that you received when you were growing up as a member of your **racial** group. Please answer the following with as many responses as you can remember as they pertain **only** to your **race**.

1. Things I was encouraged to generally believe about people who are **members of my race.**

2. Things I was discouraged to generally believe about people who are **members of my race.**

3. Ways I was taught people who are **members of my race** thought/behaved regarding school and work.

4. Values stressed to me about how a person who is a **member of my race** should behave/appear.

5. Ways I was taught to interact with people who were not **members of my race**.

© MarkCharlesGood, LLC.

First Memories of Difference

Objective: A retrospective activity to have participants practice self-awareness regarding how some of their own personal worldviews originated. It works best when followed up immediately by the "Automatics Tapes" Activity, *which is the next activity in this book.*
For: 9 – Adult
Time Needed: 20 - 30 minutes
Number of Participants: Working individually and then within small groups.
Materials Needed:
- "First Memories of Difference" worksheet (on next page).
- Writing utensil for each student.

Set Up:
Instructor speaks to the class as a large group to read directions on page and then directs them to work individually.

Directions:
Distribute: "First Memories of Difference" worksheet to the students, one for each student (on next page).
To the large group: "Please look at your "First Memories of Difference" worksheet.
- Read the directions to the students as they are written on the page. Have them work individually then have them work in small groups to share their first memories of difference and how they believe it has influenced them to this day.
- After @ 20 minutes has passed and/or it appears that every member of each small

group has had an opportunity to share their first memories of difference, tell the large group, "I hope this activity allowed you to take a look at the origin of some of your own perspectives on how you see the world today, aka, your own *worldview*.

- Then continue immediately to the "Automatics Tapes" activity.

First Memories of Difference

- Take a minute to think about your life as far back as you can remember.

- Specifically, think about the first memory you have of when you either remember yourself as being different from others or noticed someone else as being different IN ANY WAY.

- For the next few minutes, write about, think about or sketch the image of that memory to yourself on the blank portion of this paper.

- ALSO, determine how you believe that memory has influenced you to this day.

© MarkCharlesGood, LLC.

Automatic Tapes

Objective: To illustrate how our past experiences can have a significant effect on how we view the world presently in our lives.

NOTE: This activity does not have to be preceded by the "First Memories of Difference" activity if you plan to do it with students, ages 5 – 8.

For: 5 – Adult

Time Needed: 5 - 10 minutes

Number of Participants: 3 – 30

Materials Needed:
  - None for the students.
  - Teacher can use the worksheet on the next page to read aloud to the students as a large group.

Set Up:
  - Instructor speaks to the class as a large group.

Directions:

  - To the large group: "Now that you have all had a chance to share your first memory of difference and how you believe it has had an effect on you to this day, I would like to play a quick game with all of you. I am going to ask you a series of questions and I would like for you to all answer with me together.

  - DO NOT tell the students but the answer to all of the questions will be "10": Then begin with the group by asking, "What is 5 + 5? What is 6 + 4? What is 7 + 3? What is 8 + 2? What is 9 + 1?

  - Then quickly ask: "What are aluminum cans made of?"

- A number of the students will answer with, "tin" and not the correct answer which is "aluminum".

Key Points:

- <u>Point out to the group</u>: This example illustrates that as one event, stimulus or memory is created in our heads we record what might be called an *'automatic tape'*.
  - When the stimulus repeats itself in our environment we frequently turn on our *automatic tape* in order to react in the same way that we did in the past when the event first took place.
  - After a while, when the tape is turned on it is done without us even thinking about it.
  - Sometimes this is okay. At other times it can lead us to react to or give an answer, which is incorrect or even a disservice to others and ourselves.
  - As a result, it is important to take a look at our own 'worldview' as it pertains to many events or situations in our lives. By doing so, we may actually be improving upon how we see others and ourselves within our world so that it is more beneficial to us or to others to remind ourselves to "record' some new tapes every so often.

Automatic Tapes

Activity #1
Ask the large group:
- "What is 5 + 5?" (Wait for collective answer from entire group).
- "What is 6 + 4?" (Wait for collective answer from entire group).
- "What is 7 + 3?" (Wait for collective answer from entire group).
- "What is 8 + 2?" (Wait for collective answer from entire group).
- "What is 9 + 1?" (Wait for collective answer from entire group).

Then quickly ask:
- "What are aluminum cans made of?"

Activity #2
- Choose any one of the following to have them respond to and see what transpires:

Say to the large group:
You: "Say ten, ten times fast."
Them: "Ten, ten, ten, ten, ten…"
You: "What are aluminum cans made of?"
Them: (See if they respond with) "Tin."
You: (If so) "Sorry, aluminum cans are made of aluminum!"

OR

You: "Say coast, ten times."
Them: "Coast, coast, coast, coast…"
You: "Say boast, ten times."

Them: "Boast, boast, boast, boast…"
You: "What do you put in a toaster?"
Them: (See is they respond with) "Toast."
You: (If so) "Sorry, you put bread in a toaster!"

OR

You: "Say four, four times."
Them: "Four, four, four, four."
You: Now spell four, four times."
Them: "F-o-u-r, f-o-u-r, f-o-u-r, f-o-u-r."
You: "Say four, four times again."
Them: "Four, four, four, four."
You: "What do you eat soup with?"
Them: (See is they respond with) "Fork."
You: (If so) "Sorry, you eat soup with a spoon!"

Key Points:
- Any one of these examples illustrates what we call, in the subject of diversity, a concept known as an "automatic tape".
- When a stimulus or event initially occurs, each of us observes it and decides how to react or respond. As we do, a memory is essentially recorded in our heads.
- This recording is our "automatic tape."
- It is automatic because when the stimulus repeats itself exactly the same way or similar to the original stimulus, we frequently turn on our *automatic tape* in order to react.
- That automatic tape has us reacting or responding similarly to the way that we did in the past when the event first took place.

- After a while, when the tape is switched on over and over again, it is done so without us even thinking about it.
- Sometimes this is beneficial because it can be used as a mechanism for survival; like when a driver presses the brake pedal in a car while driving when seeing a traffic light turn red.
- At other times, however, it can lead us to react or respond in ways that can be a disservice to ourselves and others; such as placing an individual who we may see as part of a group in a narrow category and ultimately perpetuating a stereotype where we believe that all "members" of the same group possess all the same characteristics and follow the same behaviors.
- As a result, it is important for each of us to challenge ourselves (self-evaluation) to review our automatic tapes as they have and will pertain to many events or situations in our lives.
- By doing so, we may "record' some new tapes that help to expand our perspectives of the world around us and improve upon our own well-being and the well-being of others by doing so.

Self-Assessment Checklist

Objective:
- To determine how each of us may manage diversity or difference in our lives.
- It may be important to point out that this assessment has no bearing on whether someone is a good or bad person.
- It may be also be important to NOT have students share their results with other students but with the teacher only.
- You may wish to modify some of the questions to be more age-appropriate.

For: 14 – Adult
Number of Participants: 3 - 50
Materials Needed:
- "Self-Assessment Checklist" worksheet, one for each student (on page following instructions for this activity).
- Writing utensil for each student.

Time needed: 10 - 15 minutes
Set Up:
- Participants working individually at desks or tables.

Directions:
- Distribute the "Self-assessment Checklist" worksheet to the students, one to each student.
- Tell them that it is confidential and only you (the teacher) will see the results.
- Read the directions out loud, direct them to take their time, and then have the students begin.

- When all students are finished, explain the "score range" (below) and then collect them, if you wish.

SCORE RANGE FOR SELF-ASSESSMENT CHECKLIST

If your score is 85 or above, you probably value diversity and are able to manage people who are different from you effectively. But we always have room for improvement.

If your score is below 50, you probably have much difficulty managing diversity and could benefit from further training.

Below 85 and above 50 places you in the average range.

SELF-ASSESSMENT CHECKLIST

Use the scale below to rate how strongly you agree with the following 20 statements:

Low Agreement				**High Agreement**
1	**2**	**3**	**4**	**5**

HINT: It is very important for you to be as honest as possible with your answers so that your self-assessment is accurate. Your disclosure is meant to assist you individually and will remain anonymous from your classmates.

_____ 1. I frequently look at the things I am good at and the things I am not good at closely and make a conscious effort to improve myself.

_____ 2. I am interested in listening to the ideas of people who do not think as I think, and I respect their opinions even when I disagree with them.

_____ 3. A number of my friends and acquaintances are different from me in age, race, gender, physical abilities, economic status and education.

_____ 4. I do not need to understand everything around me. I tolerate things that are not easily defined.

_____ 5. I am able to change course quickly. I can readily change my plans or expectations to adapt to a new situation.

_____ 6. I believe that I am a product of my upbringing and that my way is not the only way.

_____ 7. I am flexible. I accept different ways of getting a job done as long as the results are good.

_____ 8. I frequently read books and magazines that cover topics with which I do not agree.

_____ 9. Given the opportunity, I frequently listen to radio shows, watch television programs or speak to individuals who have very different ideas, opinions or points of view than I.

_____ 10. I enjoy being in the company of individuals who I consider to have little in common with me.

_____ 11. I learn from the mistakes I make.

_____ 12. When I am in a situation that is unfamiliar to me, I watch and listen before I act.

_____ 13. When I am lost, I ask for directions.

_____ 14. When I do not understand what someone is saying I ask for clarification.

_____ 15. I like people and accept them as they are.

_____ 16. I am sensitive to the feelings of others and observe their reactions when I am talking.

_____ 17. I am aware of my prejudices and consciously try to control my assumptions about people.

_____ 18. I am curious about new things, people and places.

_____ 19. I often see two sides on most issues.

_____ 20. I am interested in human dynamics (relations, associations, connections, activity) and often find myself asking, "what's going on here?"

_____ TOTAL POINTS

© **MarkCharlesGood, LLC.**

Adapted from Valuing Diversity Trainer's Guide; San Francisco: Copeland Griggs Productions, Inc.

EFFECTIVE INTERPERSONAL COMMUNICATION

Trigger Terms

Objective:
- To illustrate that certain words we use may have a negative effect on oneself and on others.
- To better understand our own emotions, especially anger, and how it may disrupt healthy communication with others.

For: 5 – Adult
Time Needed: 20 - 30 minutes
Number of Participants: 3 – 30
Materials Needed:
- "Triggers" worksheet, one for each student (on next page).
- A writing utensil
- A blackboard/whiteboard, flipchart, or smartboard.

Set Up:
- Situated into small groups of no more than 6 per small group.
- Each small group should assign a recorder and a reporter.

Directions:
- Follow directions written on the top of the page of the worksheet.

Key Points:
- Ask students to define "trigger words." You are looking for a response that resembles, "Those words that make us angry."
- Point out to the large group, the importance of becoming cognizant of our "triggers" because

they directly correlate with the emotion of "anger".

- Tell them that the <u>origin of anger</u> always comes from one place, <u>our perception that we have lost control of something</u>. Whether we believe that we have no control over getting a soup dish to fit into the dishwasher to our perception that we have no control over our own lives, anger originates from this place.
- By being more acutely aware of our anger, when it arises and other emotions also, we become better equipped to resolve conflicts healthfully
- NO strategy for healthy communication will ever be fully successful unless you also take into consideration, our emotions that correlate with each situation.

TRIGGERS

Please write your responses to each of the following questions. Then share your response to each with the other members of your small group.

1. What are my TRIGGER words?

2. What kind of body language is a TRIGGER for me?

3. How do I know when I am angry?

4. How do I react to my TRIGGERS?

5. Do I have a long fuse or a short fuse?

Intent vs. Receipt: The Tennis Ball Toss

Objective: To provide an illustration of the concept of *'intent vs. receipt'*, the basic foundation of comprehending healthy communication

For: 5 – Adult

Time Needed: 5 - 10 minutes

Number of Participants:

- The instructor and 1 volunteer from the class.
- The rest of the class watching.

Materials Needed:

- 1 tennis ball or any type of soft, small ball.
- 2 participants to toss the tennis ball (1 participant is the instructor/teacher)

Set Up:

- Have the volunteer join the teacher in the front of the class.
- Give tennis ball to the student volunteer.

Directions:

- <u>Turn to the large group and state</u>: (The vocabulary may need to be modified for students of younger ages)."I would like to illustrate a basic but very important concept of healthy communication within diversity. It is called *intent vs. receipt*. Let's say that (name of volunteer) would like to send me a verbal message and that he/she wishes for me to receive or interpret exactly the way he intended. The tennis ball will represent the message. To illustrate that I have received the message in the way in which it is intended, I will need to catch the tennis ball without dropping it."

- Continue by asking the large group: "Let's say that when (name of volunteer) wishes to send me the message I am looking around and not paying attention to him. What does he need to do first?
  - Some answers could include:
    - "He needs to call out your name"
    - "She must get your attention"
- To the large group continue with: "Now that she has my attention what are some of the things she will need to do so that I have a good chance of receiving her message in the way in which she intends?"
  - Some answers could include"
    - "She needs to toss the tennis ball to you gently"
    - "He will need to toss the tennis ball in your direction"
    - "She needs to let you know that the tennis ball is coming in your direction"
- Then ask: "What is my responsibility in receiving the message?"
  - Some answers could include"
    - "You will need to do your best to catch it."
- Then have the student volunteer toss you the tennis ball:
  - Whether or not you catch it, ask the class, "Was it a guarantee that I would catch it?" The answer should be 'no.'
  - Point out that the ball represents our words. If it is thrown gently, there is a better chance that communication can be healthy. If it is thrown hard, it may hurt or create unnecessary conflict.

Key Points:

- Point out that although we can do our best to send a message in the best way possible there is no guarantee that it will be received in the way in which we intend (aka. The ball is dropped). However, the chance is far greater that it will be received correctly if we do our best to send out the message as gently as possible.
- You can follow-up by doing an activity where the tennis ball is thrown rapidly and how that may represent a message that hurts or another where the tennis ball is tossed so rapidly that it flies in the wrong direction and well past the receiver, illustrating 'a rumor'.

Understanding Anger

Objective: To provide an understanding of both the origin of anger and how we can each work to use it constructively.

For: 9 – Adult

Time Needed: 20 - 30 minutes

Number of Participants: 3 – 30

Materials Needed:
- The "Nurture the Baby" worksheet, one for each student (on the page following these instructions).
- The "Understanding Anger" and "Nurture the Baby" description for the teacher to use and/or modify, if desired.
- A writing utensil for each student.

Set Up:
- Distribute the "Nurture the Baby" worksheet to each student.
- Teacher first reading/speaking to the large group.
- Then students working together to complete the worksheet.

Directions:
- Read to the entire group: The "Understanding Anger" and "Nurture the Baby" descriptions. You may wish to modify the descriptions to be more age appropriate.
- Direct the students to first write down a description of the last time they got angry and then use that example to then work individually and complete the "Nurture the Baby" worksheet (on the next page).

Key Points:

- It will be important for students to complete step #1 of the "Nurture the Baby" worksheet by looking closely at themselves as being responsible rather than others first.

Understanding Anger:

- Anger is a normal human emotion. What is not always normal is the way in which each of us *sometimes* displays it.
- It is a big emotion, which covers many facets of our being. It is exhibited in many forms from frustration, irritation, rage, violence frequently directed outward to anger directed inward. This anger turned inward is literally the definition of *depression*. That is how big anger really is.
- All anger, no matter what its form has **one** origin. It originates from **the perception that we have lost control over something**.
- Whether you have difficulty getting the soup dish to fit into the dishwasher and it pisses you off to feeling an overwhelming and chronic rage to a sense of hopelessness and helplessness, all is based on the perception that you have lost control over something.
- Sometimes we can alleviate that anger by simply counting to ten or trying a new and better way to get the soup dish to fit in the dishwasher. But sometimes, we have no control on changing or fixing the actual stimulus over which we perceive or really have no control. No matter the depth of our anger, there is a formula we can use to help.

The Formula: "Nurture The Baby"

- If anger is present, you must immediately stop the ball toss and "nurture the baby" first before you begin the ball toss again or healthy communication will dissolve.

- Imagine this, two people having a discussion and a little baby in the next room begins to cry. This baby represents anger. The two people will not likely continue to have a conversation while the baby cries. They will, instead, pause and go nurture the baby. They might change her diaper or feed her in order stop her crying. Once that has taken place and the baby has been nurtured, the two people can then return to the other room and continue their discussion again.
- If the baby is not nurtured, what we might do is say something that could hurt someone severely, damage a working relationship or one with a student, send an email we can never get back and/or post a Tweet or Facebook status that has detrimental effects on ourselves and others.
- Anger needs to be attended to first and here are the 3 steps to *nurture the baby*.
  - Step #1: Over what do you perceive you have no control?
  - Step #2: In regard to that issue, list all the things you can control.
  - Step #3: Among your list, which is the most rational and relevant option to use at this time?

Example 1: Easiest to resolve: You become angry because the dishwasher is full of dishes and you cannot get your soup dish to fit into it. You rearrange some dishes and find a spot for the soup dish.
Example 2: Difficult to resolve: You are stuck in a traffic jam on the highway on your way home from work. The Traffic jam cannot be controlled but how you deal with it can be.
Example 3: Very difficult to resolve: You are grieving over the loss of a loved one that leads to depression. You cannot change the loss or bring the person back

but there are some things over which you do have control that can help you deal with your grief. You get a book to learn more about grief and join a support group that focuses on grieving.

"Nurture The Baby"
Please complete the following using the 3 steps to "Nurture the Baby."

Please write a brief description of the last time you got angry.

1. Step #1: Over what did you perceive you had no control?

2. Step #2: In regard to that issue, list all the things you could control.

3. Step #3: Among your list, which is the most rational and relevant option to use at this time?

© MarkCharlesGood, LLC.

CELEBRATING DIVERSITY

The Envelope

Objective: To challenge students to put into practice a sense of community service to others.
For: 7 – Adult
Time Needed: 10 - 15 minutes
Number of Participants: 3 – 50
Materials Needed:
- One envelope for each participant.
- A writing utensil for each student.
- A blank piece of paper for each student.
- Postage stamps for mailing each envelope (done one to three months later, your choice).

Set Up:
- Pass out one envelope to each participant.
- While passing out envelopes, have each student take out a writing utensil and one blank piece of paper.

Directions:
- Please write your name and address on the front of the envelope as if you were going to mail yourself a letter.
- On a blank piece of paper write the description of a personal goal, around the topic of diversity awareness, which you believe you can accomplish within the next one to three months (e.g., negative assumptions, stereotyping, being kind to someone who is different, etc.).
- When you have completed writing down your personal goal please fold up your paper and place it into the envelope addressed to you.

- Seal the envelope. The teacher will then collect each of the envelopes.
- Please await further information from the teacher.
- After collecting all of the envelopes, inform the participants that you will mail their sealed envelopes containing their personal goals to them exactly one to three months from today. When they receive it they can open the envelope and determine if they have fulfilled their personal goal. You may want to also let them know that you will not look at any of their papers. That is why they have been sealed.

Key Points: To encourage students to apply what they have learned regarding *diversity awareness* to their individual/personal lives in order to comprehend its relevance.

20th Century Figures

Objective: To urge students never to discourage others from celebrating differences by disrupting each individual's diverse personal characteristics.

For: 12 - Adult

Time Needed: 15 - 25 minutes

Number of Participants: 3 – 30

Materials Needed:
- 2 large pieces of paper or a large blackboard/whiteboard or smartboard.
- 1 magic marker or piece of chalk/dry erase marker.

Set Up: The instructor stands before the entire student body.

Directions:
- To the large group: "Let's make a list of 20th century figures who gained <u>positive</u> recognition because of their work around any aspect of diversity." **Note: You can also facilitate this activity by including "21st Century Figures" or facilitate the activity with only "21st Century Figures."**
- As the students say each name out loud, the instructor writes each on the board or on a large piece of paper with the title "20th Century" written at the top.
- After the list has been completed, ask the group, "Now let's list non-physical characteristics that all of the people on your list have in common".
- As the students name each characteristic out loud, the instructor writes each on the

board or on another large piece of paper with the title "Common Characteristics" written at the top.

- After the group has compiled the list of *common characteristics* ask: "Are there any words written on the *common characteristics* list that represent characteristics that many educators **discourage** students in our schools from exhibiting? If so, please tell me what they are and I will circle them."

- After circling all of the words, state to the large group: "Despite the fact that these are the *common characteristics* of all of the **heroes** on our "20th Century" list, take a look at how many you have indicated, are discouraged by educators in our schools. Subsequently, if this discouragement continues, how many **heroes** might educators keep from being added to our list in the future?"

Strength Bombardment

Objective: To perpetuate the importance of positive communication and to understand the difference between *confidence* and *arrogance* as they correlate with our ability to communicate.

For: 12 – Adult

Time Needed: 30 minutes

Number of Participants: 3 - 50

Materials Needed:

Breakout space.

Set Up:

Situated into small groups of no more than 5 per small group.

Directions:

To the large group:

- Direct the students to do the following within their small groups: "For the next 20 minutes, please leave this room (this is not necessary if there are restrictions from doing so. In fact, some teachers may want to supervise all groups.) and go sit in another place, take a power walk outside or go sit outside on the grass and participate in what is called a "strength bombardment."
- "Take some time to bombard each member of your group with positive qualities and characteristics you have observed in each of those persons as you have worked together."
- "You should take 3–5 minutes to bombard each individual about qualities you see in each of them that do not have to do with what they wear or what they look like but instead what

they do or who they are. Then return to this room after the 20 minutes have passed."

- While the students are out (or beforehand), write the definitions of **CONFIDENCE** and **ARROGANCE** on the board as they are written below.

After the groups return in 20 minutes:

- Ask the large group, "What was the most difficult part of this activity?"
- The overwhelming response will resemble, "accepting praise."
- Tell the students that, "The reason for this is because we do not believe we deserve it. When we are very young, we are encouraged to speak about ourselves (e.g., show and tell). But as we get older, we are discouraged from doing so as it is frequently labeled *vain* or *arrogant.* Unfortunately, this can have a negative effect on our ability to communicate effectively. Let's look at the definitions of the following two terms:"

CONFIDENCE - *A feeling or consciousness of one's powers or of reliance on one's circumstances **b:** faith or belief that one will act in a right, proper, or effective way, the quality or state of being certain.*

ARROGANCE - *A feeling or an impression of superiority manifested in an overbearing manner or presumptuous claims.*

- Continue by telling the large group, "Confidence is healthy; arrogance is not. When we are confident, we are better able to accept praise, less in need of being defined by others and more assured about our own positive characteristics. When a confident individual receives praise, she accepts it and moves on with a simple "thank you." An arrogant person will tell you that they are well aware of all of their own qualities and that you may have even missed a few. While inside, they are not genuinely assured of these qualities. An unconfident person, who is also not arrogant has much trouble accepting praise at all."

Key Points:
By being genuinely "confident" an individual is more authentic and assured about who she is and, therefore, more understanding of her own emotions so as to communicate more effectively in all aspects of her life.

Why Do We Need This Stuff?

Objective: To help students begin to practice healthy communication in answering common questions that relate to the establishment of a legitimate rationale for diversity awareness.

For: 12 – Adult

Time Needed: 45 minutes

Number of Participants: 3-50

Materials Needed:

- The "Why Do We Need This Stuff" worksheet, one for each student (on the page following these instructions).
- A writing utensil for each student.

Set Up:

- Situated into small groups of no more than 6 per small group.
- Each small group should assign one or more reporter(s).

Directions:

- To the large group: "Please turn to the page that at the top of the page reads 'Why Do We Need This Stuff?'"
- Read the directions at the top of the page to the large group, then state: "Please work in your small group to come up with your group's best answer to each of the following seven questions or comments written on the page. After all of the small groups in the class have answered all of the questions, I will give another assignment to each small group. Please take your time and answer these to the

best of your ability. You have @ 20 minutes to complete this activity."

- After all of the small groups have answered all seven questions, state: "I will now assign each small group to one or more (depending upon the size of the large group) of the questions/comments written on the page. Come up with your best *group* answer to that question/comment as you will be sharing that answer with the rest of the class. You have 1 minute please."
- After a minute has passed, state: "Okay, let's see what you have come up with." Then go over all of these questions for approximately the next 20 minutes.

Key Points:
- When completed, let the students know that this activity is very important in helping each of them to discuss the issue of diversity awareness when difficult questions about the topic emerge.

"Why Do We Need This Stuff?"

The following are some common questions/comments that may be asked/made by people in your school about the topic of diversity awareness. As you read each, please write a response(s) that you feel might help to answer them. There is not one correct answer for any.

1. "The students in our school are mostly the same. We don't really need any kind of diversity awareness."

2. "Why make things worse by stirring up this issue."

3. "We do a lot by observing Black History Month and we even have a cultural festival each year. Isn't that enough?"

4. "How does diversity even matter for us when we go look for a job?"

5. I don't see color in my school, I only see people. I like to believe that I am color blind."

© MarkCharlesGood, LLC.

Those Who Enriched the World

Objective:
- To help students to become aware of the positive contributions of LGBT people in history.
- To help students to begin to understand why mentioning the 'sexual orientation' of certain historical figures to students may be relevant and important.

For: 12 – Adult
Time Needed: 30-60 minutes
Number of Participants: 3-30
Materials Needed:
- "Those Who Enriched the World" worksheet, one for each student (on the page following these instructions). The teacher can always modify this list by adding other/different names to it, especially if there are individuals you would like to place on the list who are relevant to your specific curriculum.
- A writing utensil for each student.
- Access to the Internet for each small group.

Set Up:
- Students working together in small groups of no more than 5 people.
- Assign them to small groups based on the first letter of each student's last name.

Directions:
To the Large Group:
- Among the list of 20 individuals below, you are assigned to 5 based on the first letter of your

last name (teacher can modify the number assigned from 5 to less or more).

- Among the 5 to whom you have been assigned, please look them up on the Internet and write one paragraph about each that informs us of important characteristics of that individual which might describe their status and/or fame in current events or history.
- All of the information will be shared with the rest of the class.
- You have 30 minutes (time can be modified) to complete this assignment.

Key Points:

- Q: "What do all of these individuals have in common?"
- A: "Each of them is/was lesbian, gay or bisexual."
- Why does this matter? There are times when pointing out an individual's sexual orientation may be important or even relevant to their contribution to our world today.
- Mentioning sexual orientation has *nothing* to do with talking about sexual behavior, but instead about to whom we feel attracted or love.
- For example, imagine if we never mentioned Jacqueline Kennedy when we mention John F. Kennedy. We would still have a story but not the whole story. By leaving out this information, we may be leaving out an important part of the story.
- Yet, when it comes to people in history who happened to be lesbian and/or gay, we leave out this information frequently and often intentionally.

- Sometimes we even change the information about them in order to not discuss this. More about that later.
- If we completely exclude this information from our educational lessons, it can have a negative affect on all of our students. Please see the next PPT to learn more about what can happen when we do not mention "sexual orientation".

Those Who Enriched The World

- Among the list of 20 individuals below, you are assigned to 5 based on the first letter of your last name.
- Among the 5 to whom you have been assigned, please look them up on the Internet and write one paragraph about each that informs us about important characteristics of that individual which might describe their status and/or fame in current events or history.
- Your information will be shared with the rest of the class.

If your last name ends with A, B, C, D, E or F you are assigned to 1-5

1. Jane Addams
2. James Baldwin
3. Tammy Baldwin
4. Billy Bean
5. Willa Cather

If your last name ends with G, H, I, J, K or L you are assigned to 6-10

6. Anderson Cooper
7. Leonardo Da Vinci
8. Frederick The Great
9. Barbara Jordan
10. Buonarroti Michelangelo

If your last name ends with M, N, O, P, Q or R you are assigned to 11-15

11. Suze Orman
12. Plato
13. Eleanor Roosevelt
14. Bayard Rustin
15. Bessie Smith

If your last name ends with S, T, U, V, W, X, Y or Z you are assigned to 16-20

16. Gertrude Stein
17. Esera Tuaolo
18. Walt Whitman
19. Tennessee Williams
20. Virginia Woolf

© MarkCharlesGood, LLC.

Want More?

- For information on how to have associates from MarkCharlesGood, LLC come to your location to facilitate a Diversity Awareness training designed specifically for your organization, feel free to contact us at info@markcharlesgood.com or by phone at 610-733-9402.
- For all the services we can offer educators, schools, and school systems like yours, check out our website at www.markcharlesgood.com.

References

The Anti-Defamation League of B'Nai B'Rith. (2005) *A World of Difference Institute:* **Anti-Bias Education and Training**, Available from ADL, Washington, D.C.

The Anti-Defamation League of B'Nai B'Rith. (1994) *A World of Difference: A Prejudice Reduction Program of the Anti-Defamation League of B'Nai B'Rith*, Teacher/Student Resource Guide. Available from ADL, Washington, D.C.

Blumenfield, Warren J. *"How Homophobia Hurts Everyone" Homophobia: How We All Pay the Price* (Boston: Beacon Press, 1992) 8-13

Florida, Richard *The Rise of the Creative Class: And How It's Transforming Work, Leisure, Community and Everyday Life,* Basic Books, 2004

Florida, Richard *The Rise of the Creative Class: And How It's Transforming Work, Leisure, Community and Everyday Life,* Updated City Ranking: Basic Books, 2005

Hanh, Thich Nhat *Anger: Wisdom for Cooling the Flames,* New York, Penguin Group, 2001

Jackson, Kenneth T. *Crabgrass Frontier, The Suburbanization of the United States*, New York & Oxford: Oxford University Press, Revised 2005

McIntosh, P. "White Privilege: Unpacking the Invisible Knapsack." *Peace and Freedom* (July/August 1989): 10-12.

National MultiCultural Institute. (1994). *Developing Diversity Training for the Workplace.* Unpublished manuscript. Available from NMCI, 3000 Connecticut Avenue, N.W., Suite 438, Washington, D.C. 20008-2556.

Ogbu, John "Immigrant vs. Non-Immigrant Minorities in America." Presentation made at Prince George's County Maryland Public Schools Multicultural Education Workshop, Greenbelt, MD, August 21, 1990.

Ogbu, John Minority Status and Schooling: A Comparative Study of Immigrant and Involuntary Minorities (Reference Books in International Education, Vol 7) *Garland Publishing (August 1, 1991).*

Sue, D.W., &Sue, D., (2003) *Counseling The Culturally Diverse: Theory & Practice.* (4th ed.) (pp. 265 – 289; 439 – 455) New York: John Wiley & Sons.

Tatum, Beverly Daniel *"Why Are All the Black Kids Sitting Together in the Cafeteria?" And Other Conversations About Race*, New York: Basic Books, Revised 1999.

Zinn, Howard *A People's History of The United States: 1492-Present* Harper Perennial, Revised 2003.

Video "The Lunch Date" *DuArt Films*, 1998. 212-757-4580

NOTES

Made in the USA
Monee, IL
05 January 2021

56473829R00063